DATE DUE			

3 4880 05001209 0
Parker, Janice.

595.7
PAR

Insects

LIFE SCIENCE

INSECTS

Janice Parker

WEIGL PUBLISHERS INC.

Project Coordinator
Heather C. Hudak

Design
Bryan Pezzi

Cover Design
Terry Paulhus

Published by Weigl Publishers Inc.
350 5th Avenue, Suite 3304, PMB 6G
New York, NY 10118-0069

Website: www.weigl.com

All of the Internet URLs given in the book were valid at the time of
publication. However, due to the dynamic nature of the Internet, some
addresses may have changed, or sites may have ceased to exist since
publication. While the author and publisher regret any inconvenience
this may cause readers, no responsibility for any such changes can be
accepted by either the author or the publisher.

Library of Congress Cataloging-in-Publication Data

Parker, Janice.
  Insects / Janice Parker.
    p. cm. -- (Life science)
  Includes index.
  ISBN 978-1-59036-707-0 (hard cover : alk. paper) -- ISBN 978-1-
59036-708-7 (soft cover : alk. paper)
  1. Insects--Juvenile literature. I. Title.
  QL467.2.P339 2008
  595.7--dc22

                                    2007012622

Printed in the United States of America
1 2 3 4 5 6 7 8 9 0 11 10 09 08 07

Photograph credits: Gaye Drady from the Hunter Valley in NSW:
page 23M.

Every reasonable effort has been made to trace ownership and to
obtain permission to reprint copyright material. The publishers would
be pleased to have any errors or omissions brought to their attention
so that they may be corrected in subsequent printings.

Contents

What Do You Know about Insects?

Insects are a large group of animals that do not have a spinal column, or backbone. Many other groups of animals exist, such as birds, mammals, and reptiles. Insects can be larger than your hand or so small you cannot see them. For every person in the world, there are 200 million insects.

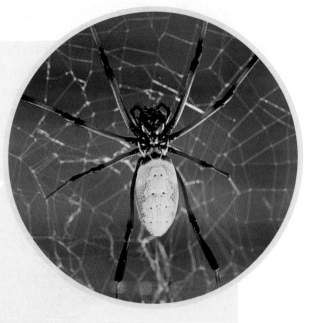

ll insects have six legs and a body
hat is divided into three parts.
he outside of their bodies is
overed by a hard skeleton
alled an **exoskeleton**.

▓ More than one
million kinds of
insects exist in
the world.

Puzzler

**Spiders are not insects.
Do you know why?
Hint: Count their legs.**

Answer: All insects have six legs—spiders have eight legs. Spiders are part of a group of animals called **arachnids**. Arachnids are relatives of insects.

Life Cycles

All animals have a life cycle. A life cycle includes birth, growth, **reproduction**, and death. Insects, like other animals, follow this life cycle.

Grasshoppers begin their lives as **eggs** buried in the ground. When an egg hatches, a **nymph** comes out. A nymph looks like a small adult without wings. Nymphs shed their skin many times as they grow. This is called **molting**. The grasshopper completes its life cycle when it becomes an adult. Adult grasshoppers have wings and can produce eggs.

sects have different types of life cles. Very simple insects hatch out of eir eggs looking just like small adult sects. These insects grow larger roughout their lives, but they always look e same. Other insects look quite different at fferent stages of their life cycle.

ome insects, such as butterflies and beetles, have four ages to their life cycle. They are egg, **larva**, **pupa**, and lult. Most of these insects begin their lives as eggs. he eggs hatch into larvae, which do not look like the lult insect. Like nymphs, larvae grow larger through olting. During the final molt, the larva surrounds itself a cover. This is the pupa stage. A butterfly's pupa called a **chrysalis**. The insect transforms into its lult shape and breaks out of the pupa chrysalis. Adult insects are le to reproduce.

Activity

Draw a Life Cycle

Draw a diagram of the life cycle of a colorful butterfly.

Types of Insects

There are many types of insects, and each one has features that make it different from others. Can you tell the difference between insects?

Types

Crickets and Grasshoppers	Leaf Insects and Stick Insects	Damselflies and Dragonflies	Termites	Cockroaches
Features				
• can jump long distances • have two pairs of wings • sing or chirp to communicate with other similar insects	• eat plants • look like sticks or leaves and can easily **camouflage** themselves in their **habitat**	• are excellent flyers • spend their early lives underwater	• can live for 10 years • only kings and queens can fly • live in large groups	• are flat with long antennae • will eat almost anything

Puzzler

What type of insect is a ladybug?

Praying Mantises	Beetles	Ants, Bees, and Wasps	Butterflies and Moths	Flies and Mosquitoes
attack and eat other insects have strong front legs	• have two pairs of wings • one set of wings covers the body in a hard shell • include fireflies	• most live in large groups • usually have two pairs of wings	• have two pairs of wings • most butterflies fly during the day • moths usually fly at night	• have one set of wings • flies are one of the fastest flying insects

Creepy-Crawly Careers

Many people work with bugs. People who study bugs are called **entomologists**. To become a professional entomologist, you must go to a university and study for a degree in science. Many different jobs involve insects. Some entomologists help farmers deal with insects that kill their crops. Others work to prevent diseases that are spread by insects. Some entomologists can even help police solve crimes by looking at insects at crime scenes.

■ **Entomologists use special equipment to study insects.**

Beetles and other insects can carry diseases to farmers' fields. These diseases can destroy large crops.

Activity

Do Your Own Research

Many careers involve insects in some way. Find out more about the different types of entomologists. Some of the types of work they do include the following.

Work with farmers to show how insects can keep their plants healthy
- Study how insects spread disease
- Find out how many insects live in an area
- Teach at universities

11

Classifying Insects

Scientists **classify** the many different type of insects into groups. Insects within each group share similar features or behave the same way.

Look for

Eyes	Legs	Antennae	Habitat
compound eyes, no eyes, simple eyes	attacking legs, digging legs, jumping legs, swimming legs	beaded, clubbed, comblike, feathery, sawlike	desert areas, human houses trees, water, underground

Activity

Drawing Insects

Think of insects that you have seen or heard about. Draw and color some of them. Group together, or classify, the insects that are similar.

Mouthparts	Color	Defense
chewing mouthparts, piercing mouthparts, sucking mouthparts, tunneling mouthparts	black, blue, brown, gray, green, white, other colors	bad smells, bites, scary appearance, spines, stingers

Helpful Insects

Some people dislike all insects, even helpful ones. Many insects are helpful to humans. Bees make honey to eat. Dragonflies eat mosquitoes. Ladybugs make a meal out of insects that destroy garden plants. Insects **pollinate** plants. Without insects, we would not have many flowers.

Some insects are admired for their beauty. Butterflies can be many brilliant colors. Many people like the sounds of crickets and grasshoppers.

■ **Ladybugs and dragonflies are helpful insects to have in a garden because they eat insects that harm plants.**

14

...sects help keep neighborhoods clean. ...hen an animal dies or garbage is left ...utside, insects often eat the remains. If ...ft to rot, these remains could make people ...animals sick.

...lkworms are a type of caterpillar. They spin cocoons out ...a very strong **fiber**. People use this fiber to make a ...autiful cloth called silk.

Activity

Use Your Five Senses to Explore Insects

You can learn about the world around you by using all of your five senses.

Listen to grasshoppers or crickets "talking" to one another. Watch a butterfly or moth flying past. Feel the sting of a mosquito.

1. Spend some time outdoors using your five senses to learn about insects.
2. Write down the names of all the insects you see, hear, or feel.
3. Paint a picture of each insect.
4. Write down which sense or senses you used to learn about each insect.
5. Taste some honey. We could not have honey without the help of bees.
6. Use your sense of smell. Can you think of any insects that can smell?

Pesky Insects

Many people are scared of insects and their relatives, such as spiders. Most insects are harmless. Even bees and wasps are dangerous only to people with allergies to their stings. Mosquitoes can carry dangerous diseases. In some regions, mosquitoes can spread a disease called malaria. Up to 500 million people get malaria every year. Malaria can cause illness unless the proper medicine is used.

■ **A mosquito's hum is the sound of its wings beating. Its wings flap about one thousand times per second.**

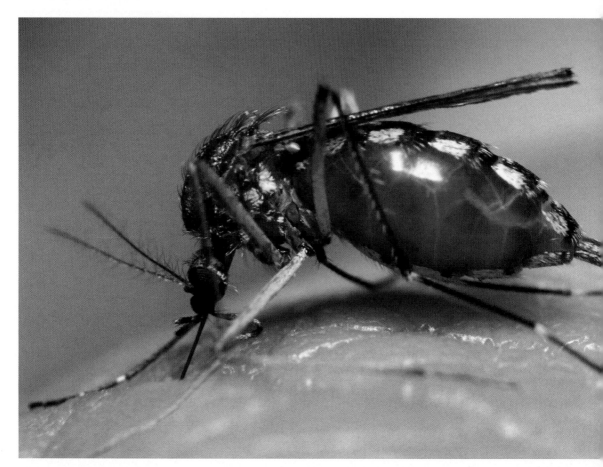

any insects can be
noying. We call
ese insects pests.
osquito bites can
ch for days. Bee and
asp stings can be very
inful. Cockroaches
pear in our homes and
read dirt. They will eat almost
ything in the house, including
oes. Insect pests can destroy
ants and crops. Certain insects
t the same plants that humans
t. They will even eat the
autiful flowers in our gardens.

■ Potato beetles and ticks are
sometimes considered pests.

Puzzler

**Do all mosquitoes
bite humans?**

Answer: No. Only female
mosquitoes suck blood from
other animals and humans. Male
mosquitoes eat only plant nectar.

Habitat

An insect's habitat is the area in which it lives. Insects live all around the world. They live in very hot and very cold areas. Insects live in water, underground, in people's homes, and even on other animals. Each type of insect has special features that help it **adapt** to its environment.

Desert Habitats

Insects that live in hot deserts must live in high temperatures with little water. Most desert insects avoid the heat by coming out only at night. During the day, they stay underground or beneath rocks. Desert insects often get water by eating plants like cactus. This keeps insects from drying out and dying.

Can you think of insects that like to live on people's heads?

Answer: Head lice. Lice live on the skin of a person's head. They lay their eggs on the hair. People must use special shampoo to get rid of lice.

Lake and Pond Habitats

Many insects have adapted to living on or water. The water scavenger beetle swims nder the water. The beetle must return to the op of the water to breathe from air bubbles. ater strider insects are able to walk on top f water. Their legs have adapted so that they o not sink into the water.

Roommates for People

Many insects live in houses and buildings with people. Houses provide some insects with a warm place to live year round. Cockroaches live in many houses. Flour beetles live in dried food goods, such as flour or nuts. Fleas make a home in the skin and fur of dogs and cats.

Now You See Them—Now You Don't!

Insects are food for a number of animals. Many insects avoid being eaten by blending into or disappearing into their habitat. This is called camouflage. A well-camouflaged insect is difficult to see. Moths that are gray and spotted often sit on tree bark during the day. These moths are very hard to see unless they move.

Some insects look like leaves or other parts of trees. Walking stick insects look like green or brown sticks on a tree. If a walking stick senses danger, it folds up its legs and falls to the ground like a dead twig.

■ Katydids have wings that look like leaves. When a katydid's wings stop moving, it is difficult to see the insect on a tree.

Most praying mantises are green and look like tree branches. The Panchong praying mantis is bright pink—just like the flowers on the trees on which it sits.

Certain insects disguise themselves by looking like other animals. These insects are called copycats. Animals avoid hover flies because they look like stinging wasps. Birds will not eat harmless viceroy butterflies. Viceroy butterflies look the same as monarch butterflies, which are poisonous.

Many insects are easy to see but are protected by their hard outer skin. Some caterpillars have sharp spines on their backs. Other animals will often drop these insects when they feel the sharp spikes. Bees and wasps will sting if they are attacked.

Activity

Find the Hidden Insects

Spend some time outside looking for insects. Look for insects that are easy to see and those that are not. Remember to look under leaves and on tree bark. If you see a rock on the ground, turn it over to see if any insects are moving around underneath.

Insect Homes

S ome insects make their own nests. These homes can have many different sections, or rooms. Insects that live in groups often have large homes.

Termite Mounds

Termites are well known for eating wood in people's homes. Some termites live in large nests made from dirt. Termites in West Africa build dirt mounds as high as 20 feet (6 meters). Up to five million termites can live in one nest. Termites build airways in the mound to help keep it cool.

Wasp Nests

Wasps build their nests out of many different materials, such as dirt and mud. Some wasp nests are made of a type of paper. Wasps make the paper by chewing up tree bark. They spit out the bark and smooth it out on the nest. The nest contains many hollow spaces inside. The largest female wasp lays eggs in the nest. Although a wasp nest looks fragile, it is very strong.

Puzzler

Honey tastes different depending on the beehive. Can you guess why?

Answer: The taste of honey depends on the plants from which the bees gather nectar. Bees that live in different places will make honey that tastes like the plants in that area.

Ant Farms

South American leaf-cutter ants live underground. They dig out large areas, or rooms. In one room, the queen ant lays eggs. In the other rooms, the ants farm their own food. The ants cut pieces from leaves and flowers and bring them to their underground nest. The plant pieces are placed in the dirt. The ants do not eat the plants. They eat the fungus that grows on the dying plants.

Egg Pots

A potter wasp builds small pots out of mud. It lays an egg in each pot. A wasp catches a caterpillar to put into each pot. When the eggs hatch, the larvae eat the caterpillar.

Beehives

Most bees live in hives. These homes are divided into many sections called honeycomb. Worker bees build honeycomb from wax that they make. The honeycomb holds all the honey needed to feed young bees. Other areas, called broodcombs, are used for eggs. Some bees live alone and build nests in holes or tunnels.

Web of Life

All living things depend on other living things to survive. Each plant and animal plays an important role in its environment. When left undisturbed by humans, plants and animals, including insects, help keep the environment in balance.

Food chains show how plants and animals survive by eating other plants or animals. Energy is transferred from one living thing to another in a food chain. A food web is many food chains that are connected to one another.

ne example of a food web starts with a plant. Tiny insects called
phids live on plants and eat the juices
om their stems. The aphids are
ten by bigger insects, such as
dybugs. Ladybugs, in turn, may
food for a bird. Many kinds of
rds eat insects. Larger animals,
ch as coyotes, eat birds.

FOOD WEB

coyote

bird

rose

aphid

ladybug

Puzzler

Many people would be happy if insects, especially mosquitoes and flies, disappeared. What would happen if insects really were to disappear?

Answer: Insects are food for many other animals, including birds and mammals. If there were no insects, many of these animals would starve.

25

Insects for Dinner

Insects are food not only for birds. Many people around the world happily eat insects. Insects are often one of the best and easiest forms of food available to people. Some people in Africa think termites are a special treat. In Bali, an island in Indonesia, people eat dragonflies. Some insects taste like nuts. Others taste like fish. Some are sweet like candy.

■ In some places, such as Mexico, insects are cooked to make a tasty meal.

ting insects is not for eryone. Many people and imals enjoy eating food ade by insects. Honey is ade by honeybees. The es collect nectar from ants and then mix it th their saliva. Bears e the taste of honey much they will allow emselves to be stung the bees to get it.

■ Beekeepers collect honey from beehives. They wear special clothes so that they will not be stung too many times.

Activity

Taste Test

Find two different types of honey. With your eyes closed, taste both. Can you tell the difference between the two?

Traveling with the Monarchs

Many insects cannot survive in cold weather. They must find warm homes for winter. Some insects live underground or stay in a nest. Others live in our warm houses. Other insects fly to a warmer habitat when winter arrives. This is called **migration**. Monarch butterflies travel long distances every year. Monarchs live in Canada and the northern United States during the summer. As the weather turns colder, the monarchs head south.

monarch butterfly may
y as far as 200 miles
20 kilometers) per day.
onarchs fly only during
e day when the weather
warm. At night, they
st on trees. Finally, the
onarchs reach their
stination in Mexico
California. This is
here they spend their
inter. The next spring,
e monarchs fly
rth again.

■ Hundreds of monarch butterflies fill
the air during migration.

Puzzler

**Monarch butterflies lay eggs as they fly north in the
spring. How do those new butterflies know where
to fly to spend their spring and winter?**

Answer: Scientists are not sure how newly born butterflies know where to
fly. By the time the eggs hatch into larvae and complete their development
into butterflies, their parents are gone. Each year, they return to exactly the
same places as their parents.

Ancient Insects

Insects have been around for a long time. Scientists know that many different types of insects lived more than 400 million years ago. Many of those ancient insects looked like insects we know today. Dragonflies looked just the same—but were much larger.

Fossils tell scientists about these ancient insects. Fewer insect fossils exist than other animal fossils. This is partly because insects have no inner bones.

ossilized bones often tell scientists
hat an animal looked like or when it
ved. Much of what we know about
inosaurs comes from finding
ossilized bones and footprints.
nlike dinosaurs, insects did not
ave behind bones. Some fossils of
sects can be found in amber.
mber is fossilized tree sap. It
oks like a clear, yellow stone.
ncient insects got stuck in the
ee sap and died. The sap turned
to amber over millions of years.
oday, those insects can still be
en in amber.

Puzzler

**Insects trapped in amber tell us how insects
looked millions of years ago. Often, scientists
have to guess what an animal looked like. Why?**

Answer: Most fossils only show the bones and footprints of an animal.
Scientists have to guess at the shape and color of an animal.

Glossary

adapt: to become suited to a certain environment or way of life by changing gradually over a long period of time

arachnids: a group of animals, including spiders, that are related to insects

camouflage: to blend in with the surroundings

chrysalis: the pupa stage in a butterfly's life cycle

classify: to arrange animals or plants into groups by comparing their features

eggs: the first stages of an insect's life cycle

entomologists: people who study insects

exoskeleton: the hard outer shell of all insects

fiber: a fine, threadlike substance

fossilized: to change into a fossil

fossils: the remains of plants or animals found hardened in layers of rock

habitat: the environment in which an insect lives

larva: the wingless stage of an insect's life cycle

migration: an animal's travels to a new area during different times of the year

molting: shedding skin and growing

nectar: a sweet liquid in many flowers

nymph: a young insect that looks like a small adult

pollinate: to carry pollen from one flower to another

pupa: the inactive stage of an insect's life cycle

reproduction: the joining together of animals to produce young

Index

Websites

www.livescience.com/insects
www.eatbug.com

www.earthlife.net/insects
www.bugwood.org/entomology.html

Some websites stay current longer than others. For further websites, use your search engines to locate topics such as bumblebees, butterflies, insects, and spiders.